Book Design by Paul Ferrini
and Lisa Carta
Inside photographs by Eugene Parulis

ISBN 9781-879159-10-5

HEARTWAYS PRESS
9 Phillips Street, Greenfield, MA 01301

Manufactured in the United States of America

The 12 Steps of
FORGIVENESS

A
Practical Manual
for Moving from Fear to Love

PAUL FERRINI

TABLE OF CONTENTS

INTRODUCTION

The Four Axioms of Forgiveness 9

FIRST CORNERSTONE

Taking Responsibility for Your Peace 16

    Step 1   Recognize the Fear 18

    Step 2   Understand that It's Love that You Want ... 22

    Step 3   Withdraw the Projection 25

    Step 4   Take Responsibility 31

SECOND CORNERSTONE

Finding Equality With Others 35

    Step 5   Release Self-Judgment and Guilt 40

    Step 6   Accept Yourself and Others as You Are ... 46

    Step 7   Be Willing to Learn and to Share 49

    Step 8   Be Your Own Authority 53

THIRD CORNERSTONE

Trusting Your Life 58

    Step 9   Accept the Lesson 62

    Step 10 See that Everything is Okay As It is 68

    Step 11 Look in the Mirror 72

    Step 12 Open Your Heart 76

FOURTH CORNERSTONE

Remembering God's Love 81

*Trials are but lessons
that you failed to learn
presented once again,
so where you made a faulty choice before
you now can make a better one,
and thus escape all pain
that what you chose before
has brought to you.*

A Course in Miracles,
Text, Page 620

PREFACE

This book contains twelve steps designed to help you shift from a fear-centered to a love-centered perception of your life. This process is not designed to eliminate fear in your life, but to help you walk through fear when it comes up.

The twelve steps contain four cornerstones. These cornerstones may be used as an abbreviated version of the twelve steps for those who find it difficult to internalize the whole process. Practice of the four cornerstones leads naturally into practice of the full sequence of twelve steps.

Feel free to stop and work on any cornerstone or step that offers you a significant challenge. Remember, it is not how many steps you practice that matters, but how deeply you practice each step. Within each step, all the other ones are contained.

This book is a practical manual. It offers you a process that needs to be worked with on a daily, hourly, indeed moment to moment basis, if it is to be a tool for transformation in your life. As such, you will find that you will get from this spiritual practice what you give to it.

Working with the twelve steps is not an intellectual process. It does not involve much if any analysis. It simply requires your willingness to remember the steps when you lose touch with your peace. That is all that you need do. This process brings you back to the truth that already resides in your heart. It simply reminds you of what you already know but have temporarily forgotten.

The twelve steps cut through the illusion of separation you create in your mind and in your relationships. They undo the false beliefs you entertain about yourself and others. They cancel out blame and shame. They give you back to yourself, to your brothers and sisters, and to the divine. This is the ongoing work of the At-one-ment.

The choice between love and fear is made every moment in our hearts and minds. That is where the peace process begins. Without peace within, peace in the world is an empty wish. Like love, peace is extended. It cannot be brought from the world to the heart. It must be brought from each heart to another, and thus to all mankind. This is the scope and manner of the work. I extend to you my love and blessings as we undertake this journey together.

Namaste.

Paul Ferrini

Introduction

THE FOUR AXIOMS OF FORGIVENESS

Forgiveness is a concept very few of us understand. We think that our biggest challenge is to forgive others for what they have done to us. But that is only the icing on the cake.

It's easy to forgive others when you have already forgiven yourself. But it's impossible to forgive others if you have not forgiven yourself.

The process of forgiveness starts in your own heart. It has very little to do with others.

When I forgive myself, it is not hard for me to forgive you. If I can remove the sting of blame and shame from my own heart, I can offer that gift to you. If I can see my own innocence, I can see yours too.

Most of us keep trying to back into forgiveness. We attempt to forgive other people before forgiving ourselves. That creates a real problem, because not everyone wants to be forgiven. Some people refuse to be forgiven! Some people even refuse to believe they are guilty!

Did you ever try to forgive someone who didn't believe he

was guilty? It's impossible! No matter how hard you try, he just won't let you.

Then, there are the people who feel guilty all the time. They keep coming up to you and begging your pardon, but you just can't bring yourself to forgive them!

Even when you realize that you are the one in need of forgiveness, you can still put the cart before the horse. You can ask some one else to forgive you, a friend perhaps, a priest or rabbi, perhaps even God. But that doesn't work either. You can be forgiven by hundreds of people, indeed forgiven by divine right, but it doesn't matter if you haven't forgiven yourself.

It just doesn't work to start outside of ourselves with this process. Starting outside is just our way of beating around the bush and beating ourselves up in the process. It doesn't open the door

---

THE FOUR AXIOMS OF FORGIVENESS

1. Forgiveness starts in our own hearts. Only when we have forgiven ourselves can we give forgiveness to, or receive it from others.

2. Forgiveness is not conditional, even though our practice of it often is.

3. Forgiveness is an ongoing process. It continues in response to every judgment we make about ourselves and others.

4. Every gesture of forgiveness is sufficient. Whatever we are able to do now is enough. This understanding enables us to practice forgiveness with forgiveness.

---

to our hearts. That door opens only when we realize that we are the ones who feel upset. We are the ones who feel guilty. We are the ones who attack and justify our attack. We are the ones who need forgiveness. And no one else can give it to us.

So the first axiom of forgiveness is that it comes from within. It's something you must do for yourself before you can demonstrate it to others.

The next axiom is that forgiveness is not conditional, nor is it partial. Forgiveness is a wholehearted, wholebeing act. It brings release from burdens, release from pain. Bargaining for forgiveness doesn't work. Yet that is exactly what we try to do:

"I'll forgive myself if I get the job or relationship I want;" or "I'll forgive you if you apologize to me first;" or "I'll forgive you, but I won't forgive him."

As long as there is some aspect of our attack we're trying to justify, forgiveness just doesn't happen. Indeed, partial forgiveness is just a subtle form of attack!

Forgiveness is unconditional and impartial. It takes me out of the past into the present. It takes me out of my self-imposed illusion of "feeling separate" into an open feeling awareness of myself and others in which intimacy is a continual possibility.

When I forgive, I accept what happened in the past, including all the past judgments I made about myself or others, without bringing this material into the present or future. Or if I bring it forward, I accept that I bring it forward, and release it.

I may "have" grievances, but I do not "hold onto" them. I understand that my grievances come from a fear space and I allow them to fall away naturally as I move through my fear and learn to trust again.

I don't have to be perfect to forgive, because forgiveness is an ongoing process in my life. I forgive, and judgment comes back, and I forgive again. There is never a time when I stop forgiving myself or others. This is the third axiom of forgiveness.

It's like the story that Samuel Beckett tells about the man who likes sucking stones. He sucks one and then puts it in his pocket and then he sucks another one. He develops elaborate schemes to make sure that each stone gets equal attention, until in exasperation he throws them all away.

Unbeknownst to us, we too keep picking up stones on our journey, pocketing them, and moving them around. They may be unnecessary burdens, as all judgments are, but we keep them till we are ready to let them go. We keep our judgments until we see how absurd our guilt/attack process is.

So we need to be patient. Forgiveness does not often happen all at once. Sometimes we throw away one stone at a time. Sometimes they all come crashing down on our toes. There is no wrong or right way. Whatever our experience, it is acceptable.

I like Beckett's metaphor much better than the one Camus gave us in The Myth of Sisyphus. Remember? The poor schmuck keeps rolling that stone up the mountain and when it's almost at the top, it falls back to the bottom, and he has to start all over again.

Of course, sometimes it feels pretty futile. We're doing the best that we can and we keep getting the same lesson upside the head for four years. But the funny thing is, that when we finally let go, the metaphor doesn't matter any more. We're content to let the big stone we've been shoving uphill lay in the gully below. Or we're happy to empty our pockets and let the little stones fall into the sand. It's all the same.

Burdens must fall away. It is their nature to be carried. And it is also their nature to be cast away. Lessons are here as long as we need them. Tell Sisyphus that, or old man Job. They don't want to hear it!

We don't want to hear it either. Today it's a problem at work; tomorrow it's a problem with our spouse or the kids. It never ends, right?

Right! Problems continue almost forever. We can't stop them from occurring. We can't tidy up the external form of our lives no matter how good we are at housekeeping. Someone always breaks an egg on the newly vacuumed carpet. Someone always spills the sauce.

What would life be like without spilling the sauce? Be honest. Would you trade this malformed, raggedy adventure in the flesh for a tidy one? Would you take rigidity if it meant neither pain nor humor, neither struggle nor learning?

Be honest. There is something here worth preserving. Beneath the mountains of dogdew, there is grass growing. There is sunlight and shade and rivers flowing. There is love beneath the pain. And love is what we want.

This book is about going through the pain to get to the love, living through the darkness to get to the light. We don't say ignore the darkness. We don't say forget the light. We say take them together. Take yourself together with all your contradictions. That is what the healing journey is all about.

Why do we need forgiveness? Because every one of us has condemned ourselves. And every one of us has tried to work out of our self-hatred by projecting the responsibility for our problems onto others.

But it just doesn't work. Self-hatred remains self-hatred, even when other people become involved. Attacking others or defending against their attack does not lessen our deep-seated judgment of ourselves. Deep down inside every single one of us is a wounded child who needs to heal.

The process of forgiveness offers this child the opportunity to heal. It is a life-long process that continues as long as we continue to judge ourselves or others.

We aren't going to stop judging right away, but we can begin to learn how we are wounded by the judgments we make. And, through self-acceptance, we can bring love to those wounded places within. Every act of acceptance neutralizes some judgment we have made.

Every act of acceptance opens our heart to love. And love heals all wounds.

As we move through life, many situations occur and many relationships are offered to us. Each one offers an opportunity to choose fear or to choose love. If we choose love, we bless ourselves and others. If we choose fear, we cry out for love from all our woundedness. Every apparent attack, is a call for love. Every crisis in life is a call to healing.

No thought or action, regardless of how ill-conceived it is, condemns us to eternal suffering. For right now, in this moment, we can make a new choice.

If Jesus could choose to love the very people who were pounding nails into his body, if He could see the face of Christ in them, how can we fail to see it in one another? The life of Jesus is a powerful teaching for us, not just because it shows us the light, but because it also shows how we can bring the darkness to the light.

14

Jesus did not tell us to deny our fear. He showed us how to walk through it. Don't think he was a stranger to temptation or doubt. He spent forty days in the desert. He cried out on the cross "Lord, why have you forsaken me?" He was human. He had a body.

He felt pain.

You cannot say that he did not know the depths of suffering. He did. But in the face of all that, he chose to love and to forgive. That is why he is such a powerful teacher for us.

But this book is not about the specialness of Jesus, or anyone else. It is about a process that each of us must go through to find the source of peace. As such, we learn from every brother or sister who makes the journey with us.

FIRST CORNERSTONE

Taking Responsibility for Your Peace

When you take responsibility for your peace you understand that you are the cause of whatever you think or feel. Other people seem to impact on your happiness or sadness, but your belief that others are responsible for your life in any way is just an appearance, a distortion on the surface which veils the real substance. This is the illusion of which *A Course in Miracles* speaks. It is not the true reality.

To be sure, every one of us has a tendency to look outside of ourselves for satisfaction. And we also have a tendency to blame others for our problems. Seeking the source of joy or the source of forgiveness outside inevitably lead to disappointment. Neither one exists outside our own hearts and minds.

When I can find joy within, my joy is unconditional. It does not depend on other people living with me. It does not depend on other people loving me. It does not even depend on other people liking me or treating me fairly. My joy is a deep confidence I have in myself that says "I know I'm okay as I am." It is an existential affirmation of my being that can only come from me.

Similarly, when I can find forgiveness within, the only change that is necessary in my life comes from within. I don't have to try to change you. I don't have to change any outer aspects of my life. Forgiving myself brings release, for it is unconditional. It says: "I acknowledge my mistake and I learn from it. My mistake does not condemn me. I accept the lesson and let the judgment go."

There is never a conflict situation in my life which I cannot bring to peace through forgiving myself. Forgiveness of others is always superficial. Self-forgiveness goes deeper. It becomes a way of taking responsibility for my life right now.

Properly speaking there are only three states of consciousness available to us. One is love, which is eternal and unconditional.

One is fear, which is temporary and conditional. And the last is forgiveness, which is a bridge from the illusion of fear to the reality of love.

Moving from fear to love means recognizing my fear when it comes up and moving through that fear. It means recognizing my judgment when it comes up and working through that judgment. It means hearing my own call for love and learning to answer it.

There are aspects of the journey which are solitary in nature. They have to do with recognizing my ultimate responsibility for everything that happens in my life. They have to do with coming to accept myself existentially. Until I do that, I cannot make peace with my brother or sister, and I cannot make peace with God.

So the first major movement in the three-phase process of forgiveness is self-acceptance. It is self-forgiveness. It is self-responsibility. It is claiming my life now, in its totality, exactly as it is, without judgment. It is loving myself moment to moment. It is being my own supply.

STEP 1

Recognize the Fear

We begin this journey together by recognizing the fear, the sadness, the pain, the hurt, the envy, the anger, the feelings of separation. We don't seek to justify these feelings, nor do we condemn them. We just allow ourselves to be aware that they are there. The following process can help us be with our feelings without running away from them (denying them) or externalizing them (projecting them).

- We recognize the feeling.
- We do not justify or condemn what we are feeling.
- We accept the feeling and give ourselves permission to feel it.
- We allow the feeling to speak to us.
- We honor it as an inner communication.
- We take responsibility for the feeling. e.g. "I feel hurt, angry, sad, etc."

- We refuse any inclination to make any one else responsible for what we feel. We stay with the feeling.

- We refuse to intellectualize the feeling. It is not important to know "why" we feel the way we do.

- As we stay with the feeling, we become aware that we are not being very loving right now, toward ourselves or others.

- We allow this message to sink in, staying with the feeling until it begins to shift.

It is important to realize that every negative feeling stems from the perception of a lack of love. Ultimately, that love must be supplied from within. That is why we don't want to look outside of ourselves. We don't want to move away from the feeling, but into it. We want to face the fact that we want love and we don't feel loved or loving. We want to be with that emptiness, that apparent lack.

Being with that emptiness helps us get behind it. It helps us understand or stand under it. That is where we find the love we think is missing.

The source of love is not shallow. It goes down deep in the heart, as deep as our suffering is. Divine Mother hides in the black pit. We have to go into that pit to find Her. We have to go through our fear, our anger and our shame to feel Her unconditional love for us.

That is our descent. It is one half of our journey. We can't embrace love until we learn to be with our fear and our feelings of separation. We have to come to terms with where we are emotionally.

To pretend not to be upset when we are upset is baldersnatch. Yet we do it all the time.

"I'm not upset." (denial)

"You're the one who is upset." (projection)

Why is it so hard for me to admit to myself or to you that I am upset, that in this moment I am overwhelmed by fear? Do I think that I am the only one who has such an experience?

Apparently I do. Apparently you do. Apparently we're both trying to impress each other, when what we really need is a good hug.

One of us just has to have the guts to say: "Wow, I feel really scared right now." And the other one will probably say "Me too."

But I think he's going to say "I told you so, you stupid idiot; it's all your fault." And that's why I don't say how I feel.

So it's always hard to release each other from the denial. Illusion is built out of denial. It's a foundation poured on quicksand. It starts with a simple misperception and ends with a complex one.

Once there is a single attack, all the other attacks follow, each one justifying his attack as defense. The Tower of Babel is made out of fear-based assumptions.

So, we agree to feel the fear, because the denial of our own fear is where illusion gets its foothold. All the inequities of the world stem from this denial in our minds.

Feeling our fear and acknowledging it is a moment when we experience equality with all our brothers and sisters. It is a moment when we are all innocent, all free to choose, all rooting for each other.

That moment is brought to us continually. We understand that every choice is a choice between love and fear, but we can't begin to access our love until we acknowledge our fear.

As you will see, as you move through the steps in this book, the balance gradually begins to shift from fear to love. Yet even here, where all of us must begin, love is present.

In this step, we remove the first barrier to love's presence. No, that barrier is not fear. It is denial of fear.

The first step of forgiveness is to give ourselves permission to be afraid and to feel all of our feelings. We cannot move though our fear if we are afraid to experience it.

That is the moment when we take up the cross and walk up the hill, as our elder brother did. Feeling the fear, we walk through it, with love calling us, a gentle promise in the skies of early morning.

STEP 2

Understand It's Love that You Want

I think that I want more money, or more sex, or more recognition, or better health, but it's love I really want. I think that I will be right if I prove you wrong, but it's love I really want. I think I'll feel better if you are punished for your sins, but it's love I really want.

All I really want, my friend, is for you to love me. If I was sure of your love, the rest would be okay. Somehow, I would find a way to accept the rest and work with it.

Those of us who have looked for perfection have had to learn the hard way that it just does not exist. Other people are not here to make us happy. They are here to help us learn. Beneath this dimly remembered goal there is the memory of a love that binds us all.

We are here to love and to learn. We are not here to force learning or loving, but to let each lead naturally to the other. When one is present, the other is as well.

So life doesn't always go my way. Sometimes I want you to please me and you are in my life to help me wake up. You are here to help me learn to take responsibility. We do this dance where I keep trying to get you to give me what I want and you keep dancing away. I begin to think that you don't love me. I begin to resent you. I feel angry because I think you intentionally refuse to meet my needs.

But you are not here to meet my needs. You are here to show me my needs so I can learn to meet them myself. This is your purpose and when you fulfill it, you set us both free.

You know, I think I want you to meet my needs, but that's not really true. I want you to meet your needs. I want you to be happy. I just need to know that, if you move away from me, you're not rejecting me. I just need to know that you love me.

When I know that, I don't want to stand in your way. In fact, I'll open the door and wish you well.

I don't want to be the person who keeps you against your will. And I don't want to be kept against mine.

I know that we are all free to choose. I just need to know that, whatever choice you make, you still love me.

That is what my child needs. And even though I keep getting older, that child does not go away. If anything, he just gets bigger and bolder in my heart. He learns to ask for what he needs.

He is no longer ashamed to ask.

He used to try to manipulate and control and badger to get his way. But that was because he wasn't listened to. Now that he knows that I listen, he just asks for very simple things. "I just need to know that you love me."

In my pain, my confusion, my hurt, my sadness, I just need

to know that I am loved. If I know I'm loved, the pain begins to fade. The separation is gradually bridged.

Something happens when I know that I'm loved. But it can't happen until I know that love is what I want and I have the courage to ask for it.

My feelings are an inner communication to me that I am not feeling loving toward myself and others. I have over- or under- extended myself, allowed myself to be stepped on or stepped on someone else's toes. I am not feeling loved. I am not feeling loving.

That is what I must recognize. And then, when I recognize it, I must decide that love is what I want. I cannot continue on the journey of forgiveness unless right now I decide that love is what I want.

Yes, it's okay to feel my pain, but feeling my pain just tells me that love is what I want. Feeling separate, angry, envious, guilty, sad just tells me that love is what I want.

The incredible thing is that when I do not justify or condemn my feelings they lead me to an emptiness that can only be filled by love. And that love always begins in my own heart.

Your love may join with it, but I cannot depend on your love. Love enters when I begin to love myself. And love enters when I begin to love you.

So Step Two helps me recognize that I want love and I can give it to myself. That recognition sets the next one in motion.

STEP 3

Withdraw the Projection

I n Step One, I learned to be with my feelings, yet I still have a tendency to think that you are the cause of how I feel. In Step Two, I learned that love is what I want. Yet I still have a tendency to look to you for love.

My old pattern is to make you responsible for how I feel. My old pattern is to ask you to fix things for me, or to try to fix them for you. My old pattern is to accuse you of not loving me enough, which is just another way of trying to make you responsible for my need for love.

So my next psychological movement is to know that love is what I want but I cannot depend on you to give it to me. Perhaps you will, perhaps you won't, but I can't do anything about your choice. If I try to influence you by putting you under pressure or making you feel guilty, I will just decrease the possibility that you can love me authentically.

If I want your love, I must set you free. I must be willing to do without it. I must be willing to look for love within, not without.

That sounds very nice, but it's a lot harder than it sounds. It means I have to go back inside that black hole in my heart and find the light that's hidden there. I must search through the dark caverns of all my woundedness to find the tiny light of self-affirmation that burns within.

I thought this forgiveness thing would be a lot easier. I'd just realize that love is what I want, and I'd ask for it, and it would just come to me on a white horse in the shape of a prince or princess. Now I find out that that too was an illusion.

Instead, I'm asked to be a coal miner, to put on protective garments and to descend into the belly of the earth to find this light I'm supposed to have. I'm not so sure I really believe that it's there or, if it is there, I'm not sure I can find it. I was willing so long as there was a guarantee, but now that the guarantee has gone out the window, I'm not so sure that I'm willing.

I thought the descent was over. Please, have a heart! Can't I just skip this step and move on to the next?

Sound familiar?

If I don't get what I want, then I'm not sure I'll buy this teaching. Job had the same problem, in reverse. Every time he thought he'd finally got it together and pleased God, he got wiped out.

Our tendency is to look for confirmation outside ourselves. And when it doesn't come, or when new trials come instead, we either feel that we are failures or that we were foolish to have faith in a higher power to begin with.

If I ask for love and you love me, I think that I am done with my spiritual work. I thank God that I am so blessed that I could complete in two steps what others must take twelve steps to complete.

Maybe that's why the cosmic clock doesn't always agree with us about our personal timetables or desires! There's still more work to do. Because one day, all that is outside of us won't be there to confirm our experience.

We have to know truth inside our own hearts. We have to find love where it begins, not where it ends.

So sometimes our desires and plans are thwarted, indeed even bashed to pieces. And every goal we had and everything we thought we were about is demolished before our eyes. And we sit there, as Job did, numb and speechless. "Just what do you want from me, Lord?"

The old answer was: "I want you to do fifteen Hail Marys, kiss one hundred elephant bums, and make a donation to the Lord's cause." We're wise to that one now. Too many elephant hairs in our faces, I guess!

After Jim Jones, Ragneesh, Jim Baker, Swami Rama, and Werner Erhard, we've fortunately become a little skeptical about outside authority! (Hey, nothing against these guys; they were here learning the same lessons as the rest of us.)

Sooner or later we find out there's no one else out there who has the answer for us. But until we find that out, we have to keep getting knocked in the third eye, or the third leg, as the case may be.

So even if you don't love me, I'm still here. I can't really change that. Even suicide can't really change that, because wherever I am, I am. The form of my existence is not what's important. The content determines the form. And as long as I have a certain misperception about reality, I will attract a correction to that misperception.

Being free has nothing to do with leaving the body. Being free means letting go of what isn't true. If that can't happen in the body, then it can't happen anywhere else, because the body is just a form that comes and goes.

So, here I am. And the only way I get my life jump-started is by accepting my life exactly as it is, by accepting myself and you exactly as we are. That is the place where my heart opens. That is the place where love begins.

When I withdraw my projection from you, I understand that what I like or dislike about you is completely irrelevant to what I am here to learn. If I like you, I think you are here to be my partner and helpmate. If I dislike you, I feel that you are here to torment me. These beliefs are really the same, just different ends of the spectrum.

One movement brings desire. The next brings fear. These two move like a seesaw throughout our lives. Because desire is fueled by the belief in special relationships, all forms of desire are based on a perception of lack.

I lack something in myself; therefore, I need you to provide it. You see, it is fear-based. And if my desires are not satisfied, then I become angry or hurt. The cycle of fear continues.

We like to elevate desire to the spiritual level. We talk about the "desire for God." That is a non sequitur. Wherever desire is, attachment is, and there is no room for God. God comes to an empty seat, not to a full one.

The flame begins in our own hearts. The relationship with

God begins in the depths of loneliness and yearning. The awareness of God's presence happens when we know that we are not going to find satisfaction outside ourselves.

You see, I must come to understand that there is nothing that you can give to me that I do not already have. And there is nothing that you can take away from me that I really have to begin with.

Everything you give to me is illusion. Everything you take away from me is illusion.

What I have, you also have. What I do not have, you do not have either. That is the divine structure of creation. It is based on complete equality. Any deviation from that existential equality is a perversion we have introduced.

We cannot come back into harmony with the divine plan until we look behind our own illusions. Only then will we see what's real.

It is a difficult fact — but we have to face it so we might as well begin now — that my only proper relationship with any human being is one of brother or sister. Call that human being Jesus, or call him Hitler. One is not more my brother than the other.

The part of me that condemns Hitler condemns myself and all my brothers and sisters for their mistakes. This is one gesture of the illusion: to create scapegoats, to deny responsibility for bringing our own darkness to the light.

And the part of me that raises Jesus up onto a pedestal is the part that would find myself and others inadequate. I believe that because Jesus walked through his fear I don't have to walk through mine. Bullsquatos! Because he walked through his fear, he showed me that I am capable of walking through my own fear.

Whenever we raise or lower someone else we make that basic gesture of inequality that covers up the truth. Whenever we think that someone else has the answer for us, or we believe that someone else is preventing us from realizing our potential, we buy into the illusion.

None of that is real. Always, there is just you and me. We are equals, but do not often perceive ourselves that way. Every deviation from equality is a strange and sometimes intriguing dance, but it always brings us back face to face, where we are now.

I finally get step three when I recognize that it's all up to me. I am the channel for love in the world. Only then is my call for love answered. For as I open to love, I extend it, and as I extend it, it returns to me.

STEP 4

Take Responsibility

One of the ways I begin to love myself is to begin to take responsibility for my life exactly as it is. Whatever I see on the outside is just a reflection of what is within.

I get into trouble only when I cannot accept my life as it is. Sometimes I reject certain people and situations. Sometimes I hang onto certain people and situations. Both rejection and attachment indicate lack of acceptance.

My acceptance of my life does not mean that it will not change. Surely it will. Sometimes that change will be anticipated. Sometimes it won't.

Change will come as it is needed. But right now my challenge is to be with what is. Is there pain? Okay then I must be with the pain. Is there sadness? Okay, then I must be with the sadness.

There is no "supposed to" in life. There is just what is happening. And that is always enough. If it seems not to be enough, or perhaps to be too much, it is because we perceive it that way.

Our beliefs are just ways of seeing. They almost always require correction, because we almost always see out of desire or fear.

A most important spiritual practice is to just let things be as they are without interpretation, without embellishment, without judgment. That immediately gives the ego a coronary. Imagine telling the ego not to judge, compare, interpret? What then is it to do? It doesn't really know how to do anything else.

So the practice becomes watching the ego go through its judgments and interpretations, not stopping the ego from going through them. Because as soon as one tries to stop the ego from judging, a new level of judgment begins.

So we just accept the fact that the ego is doing its number and watch it. That's the hurt child in all of us crying out for attention. It wants love, but does not know how to ask for it. And it goes on badgering forever!

It's okay. Do you hear that folks? It's okay to be in ego, because we all are in ego! Ninety percent of the time, we're coming from desire or fear (and as we've said desire is just another form of fear). There's nothing to be ashamed about. We all do it.

Acknowledging where we are allows us to witness it. Witnessing is just being present watching the mind dance around in the air. It's not going to stop dancing until we let it play itself out. So watching becomes a spiritual practice, a practice of deep compassion for ourselves and others.

You see, what we have is what we have. We're not supposed to get rid of any of it. And we're not supposed to add to it either.

We just need to be with it till we come to understand it. The more we understand desire and fear the more we become free of their compulsions. It's not something that we do. It's just something that happens naturally through our practice.

We have to remember that our goal is not to change the world or even ourselves. Our goal is to change our perceptions about the world and about ourselves. Our goal is to see with the eyes of love instead of the eyes of fear. This involves a different way of looking, a more objective way of looking, a way of looking without being attached to what we see.

That is our spiritual practice. It is one we share with many traditions.

So taking responsibility means accepting my life as it is. That means I don't waste my energy trying to change the eternal form of my life. It means that I don't look to others to provide the motivation for change. If change comes at all, it comes from within. It comes from being with what is here and now with patience and integrity.

The best way to confront a negative situation is not to run away from it but to walk right through it. It's only negative because I've forgotten my innocence and my brother's or sister's. Why let myself be put off by my fear and that of others?

Nothing I see means what I think it does. Nothing I see means anything. Fear begins with interpretation, with memory of the past. Yet each moment is whole and free. In each moment, my choice is reborn.

It does not matter how many mistakes I have made. I do not carry them with me, although I may believe I do. Each moment

I am free to choose. I am free to take responsibility for my life.

Let me go ahead with patience and faith. If I walk down a certain path, I am meant to find where it leads. Even if it comes to a cul de sac, I have lost nothing. No path is the final path, yet every path brings a lesson that must be learned. When all lessons are learned, the need for a path disappears. The need for a form dissolves.

It's okay. I am in ego and I create moment by moment out of desire or fear. That is the way it is. I take responsibility for it. I don't need to change anything. I just need to be aware of what's happening.

SECOND CORNERSTONE

Finding Equality with Others

The key to finding our equality with others lies in our individual practice of taking responsibility. As long as we are taking responsibility for our own lives, we do not place inappropriate expectations upon others or unnecessary burdens upon ourselves.

Yet inevitably, just as I make mistakes in my own practice, I make mistakes in my relationships. I take too much responsibility here, and not enough there. I overextend here, and I underextend there. I decide for you when you need to decide for yourself. And I let you decide for me when I need to make my own decision. The boundaries that naturally assert themselves when both people are being responsible begin to blur. Abuse and co-dependence result.

I find myself constantly losing my sense of equality with others. Here I am raised up. And there I am brought down. Neither position feels right. I want to see face to face. I want mutuality, fairness, equality. Yet the only way I can find it is to take responsibility for what happens when I don't.

In this moment I feel wounded by you, but I realize that you are not the cause of my woundedness. My wound existed before you reached out and touched me in that sensitive place.

Or I feel angry at you because you have disappointed me. Yet you are not the cause of my disappointment. My expectations of you program me for rejection. You just happen to pass through my program. You appear as a mirror to show me that my expectations are dysfunctional. I can't change what you do or don't do, but I can change my expectations of you.

I cannot change you. Therefore my only stance toward you must be one of acceptance. Whenever I don't accept you as you are, I lose my peace.

Jesus said, "do unto others as you would have them do unto you." This is a primary spiritual practice, as important as is taking responsibility for your life.

If you judge others, you disturb your peace, because every judgment you make is internalized. If you accept others, you bless yourself, for what you put out returns to you.

The important thing to understand is that every thought returns home. Projection is an illusion. I can hate something in you, but that hatred remains in me. I think it goes to you, but it only does if you take it. If you don't recognize my hatred, it doesn't stick to you.

Every thought returns home. I cannot face you because I cannot face myself. I think you are reprehensible because I am not ready to deal with my own shame.

Every reaction to another person in my life is a mirror for me. Whatever I see in you that I don't accept tells me what I'm unwilling to accept about myself. Whatever I expect from you that you can't give tells me what I need to give to myself.

Every relationship presupposes a context for learning or a context for self-crucifixion. When I see myself in the mirror of your eyes, I give myself permission to grow. When I find limitations in you, I refuse to step beyond my own self-doubt.

I will always use you as an excuse for why I can't grow. But that will not change anything. My growth remains my responsibility, no matter how much I try to shift that responsibility to you.

If you are foolish enough to accept a responsibility that does not belong to you, it can only mean that you too must learn to take authentic responsibility for yourself. Aggressive and passive partners have the same lesson. They just play out opposite ends of it. And, as we know from the Taoist wisdom, opposites are not as far apart as we think.

So finding my equality with you is an exercise in losing it, and losing it is an exercise in finding it. If you don't believe this, ask yourself "How could I find it if I hadn't lost it?" There would be nothing to find, no sense of loss. And if there is a sense of loss, it must come from a memory of a time when no loss was felt. "How could I lose it if I never had it?"

Equality is real. Inequality is not. Yet it is through inequality that I learn about equality. When I really understand equality, I realize it was always there. I never lost it. I just thought that I did.

Thinking I've lost it and realizing that I haven't represent the full spectrum of forgiveness, from the first step of recognizing that I am upset to the last step of opening my heart to the peace that's always there. I know I am finally forgiven when I realize that there is nothing to forgive. *A Course in Miracles* says it like this: "Nothing real can be threatened. Nothing unreal exists."

I never lose my innocence, nor does my brother or sister. We just appear to lose it, for a moment perhaps, for a day or two, perhaps for a whole lifetime. The length of time does not matter. For when we wake up, the dream is forgotten.

Remaining in illusion does not make you bad. It just continues your suffering. When you are ready, you let that suffering go. And once you do, it doesn't matter whether you've had it for two minutes or for ten years. It no longer exists.

Bringing this understanding to our relationships is not easy. Just as we are invested in the physical attributes of the world and our perceptions of them, so we are invested in our relationships and all the emotions they stir up in us. We are not ready, perhaps, to see all this as a dream of inequality, yet that is what it is, whenever we are upset.

All our pain is a result of seeing something that isn't there. We think it's there because our ideas and beliefs seem to stick to certain people or situations. We think that gives those ideas credibility because now they are housed in a relationship. But it just thickens the plot and brings in a new cast of characters.

So we need to acknowledge the fact that we are directing our own movie here. And what we see on the screen out there is just a reflection of the contents of our own consciousness.

Nevertheless, we must realize that ours is not the only movie being made. Those same people who appear to be actors or technicians in our movie are simultaneously directing their own movie in which we are the characters or camera person. If you've ever seen the movie Rashamon by Akira Kurasawa, you've witnessed this concept expressed with great lyricism and compassion.

There may be no ultimate boundaries between us, but it is impossible for us to join together unless we acknowledge the boundaries of our own experience and honor the experience of other people. We do not have to agree with each other. But we do have to respect each other. Consensus, to the extent that it is possible, comes out of the atmosphere of mutual respect.

Without mutual respect, which means "healthy boundaries," consensus is inevitably forced. And "forced consensus" is as ridiculous as it sounds.

Finding our equality with one another means recognizing that there are many ways of looking at any situation and we have only one of them. Listening to others, respecting their ideas and experiences, helps to open us to a wider spectrum of reality. It enables us to open up the doors of our conceptual prison and walk free into the light of day. It helps us understand the limits of our knowledge so that we can move into the unknown, alone and together.

STEP 5

Release Self-Judgment and Guilt

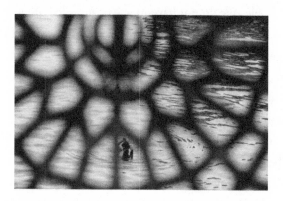

Whether I know it or not, I'm always attacking myself. I may believe that I'm attacking you, but that's just an illusion. Of course, sometimes you buy into the illusion too, and then you take offense. That's how the world turns.

But, in truth, I cannot attack you. I can only attack myself. Everything that I project onto you comes home to me. Thought is a perfect boomerang. It always returns to the one who sent it out.

It doesn't have anything to do with punishment! Many people, even those who believe in karma, don't understand that. Nobody is being punished for his sins. He's just getting back what he put out so that he can become aware of it. If he puts out anger, anger comes back to him, because he needs to become responsible for his anger. He must own everything he puts out. Only by owning it, will it be released.

It's a simple law. We don't have to beat each other with it. We don't have to say "There you go, you creep. I knew you'd get yours back." We don't have to play God. We're not needed for that role.

We just need to understand that we are going to keep on making mistakes until we learn our lessons. We are going to keep on projecting negative and positive qualities onto others so long as we are unwilling to own them in ourselves. We are going to keep on attacking others until we own the attack.

Owning the attack is just a way of short-circuiting the process. I say: "Okay, anger, I know you belong to me, so I'm not going to pretend that you belong to someone else." That doesn't mean that I don't express the anger. If it's there, it's my responsibility to express it. But I must do so knowing it belongs to me. That way it does not have to go out, stick to someone who feels guilty enough to pick it up, and then come back to me through some form of quiet resentment.

I take responsibility for the anger. I understand that it is not you, but me whom I attack. I don't get lost in the projection, or at least I don't when I am successful.

Success doesn't happen all the time or all at once. Sometimes I attack you, and sometimes I own the attack. When I attack you, I feel guilty, because I believe that I can hurt you. I carry that guilt around, and then when you or someone else attacks me, my guilt invites the attack to stick. It's all very bizarre.

Whenever I strike out at you I feel terrible. That establishes me as a target for attack. Strangers with stored up anger sense a potential victim coming when I pass by. Even German Shepherds pick up the scent!

Every time I attack you I establish my own guilt. If you don't think this is true, read Dostoevsky's *Crime and Punishment.* In the novel, Roskolnikov tries to create the perfect crime. He believes that if he kills "for a good reason" he will not feel guilty about it. It doesn't work.

True, he isn't caught. He gets away with it. But he can't live with the guilt. Eventually, he turns himself in.

That's what we all have to do: turn ourselves in. As soon as we attack, we need to remember that we are establishing our guilt.

Let's fess up right away. To hell with justifying our actions! We know attack cannot be justified. So let's just take responsibility for bringing healing to ourselves and others.

"I made a mistake, brother. I attacked you because I was afraid. I thought I had a right to attack you, but I was wrong. Forgive me. Help me get back on track."

When I make my attack a call for love, my brothers and sisters allow me to approach them. This is a gesture of reconciliation.

If I recognize my attack and take responsibility to correct it, I do not establish my guilt. Guilt is established when I justify my attack and refuse to make amends.

Chronic guilt is nothing more than the consistent refusal to take responsibility for recognizing and learning from my mistakes. Nobody becomes a punching bag without cause. Yet often the cause is hidden deeply in the psyche.

Every attack I make on you is an attack on myself. That attack can be a very subtle form of judgment, yet if repeated over and over it continually gives me the message that I am inadequate.

It is not coincidence that those individuals who have the lowest self-esteem are the same people who make the greatest number of judgments of other people. The more we judge others, the more we subconsciously judge ourselves.

All projections return home. That is the function of guilt. On some level, it refuses to let our attack leave us. We simply can not attack others without feeling responsible for the attack on some level of our being.

When we make this responsibility conscious, we can begin to heal. When we allow it to remain unconscious, we attract events which force us to become conscious not only of our trespasses against others, but of the deep self-hatred behind them.

Guilt and responsibility are mutually exclusive. Guilt holds onto the wound and so prevents it from healing. Responsibility is the first step in the healing process.

To let go of self-judgment and guilt, we must begin to take responsibility for our attack against others. We must become conscious of our projections as they happen.

Becoming conscious of our attack, we see the cause behind it. We see our own fears, our deep-seated judgments and feelings of inadequacy. We see our deep call for love.

That is essential. We cannot begin to forgive ourselves until we realize that all of our darkness is a call for light, and all our anger and hurt is a call for love. We need to acknowledge this, or we will take our awareness and use it to beat ourselves.

We mustn't underestimate the danger of this! If we give our healing process over to the ego, it will be another wounding process. Only Spirit may be in charge of our healing, for Spirit affirms us at the same time that it encourages us to make amends and learn from our mistakes.

I am not evil because I attacked you, nor are you evil because you attacked me. Our attack on each other comes from a deep sense of inadequacy in both of us. It comes from a place where neither you nor I feel loved.

Recognizing this is the beginning of the call to grace. It is the beginning of seeing, even in the darkness, with the eyes of love.

So long as I crucify myself or you for making a mistake, our healing cannot begin. It is not the mistake that matters. It is the learning, the growing, the change in perception that the mistake brings up.

When I see that, I make my lessons okay. I make your lessons okay. I have a ground to proceed on. Reconciliation and reconstruction begin on this ground. This is the true foundation of healing, in forgiveness of all mistakes and in gratitude for the awarenesses they bring.

Remember, responsibility does not come from the ego. Guilt does. Guilt continues the sense of separation. It keeps the wound open.

Guilt says: "Nothing I do will ever be enough to make amends for my wrongs."

Responsibility says: "I opened this wound and I can close it."

It is important to know the difference.

Many new age ideas have been taken up by our egos as tools not for growth, but for punishing ourselves and others. Many people who got really sick had to listen to drivel like: "You made yourself sick. It's your anger that gave you cancer. You aren't healing because you're still holding onto your anger." Talk about a guilt trip? That's just the ego trying to run the "responsibility tape." It doesn't work.

When Spirit is in charge of the responsibility program it makes everything all right. It makes this place of cancer or whatever it is a place to be and grow from. It doesn't measure progress with external standards. It just says: there is a place within where peace can be found.

When we are talking about healing, we are talking about the release of self-judgments and guilt over the mistakes of the past. It involves responsibility and gentleness. It is a letting go of what doesn't belong to us.

It is a washing clean of the sticky substance that appeared on our skin when we proceeded to justify our judgments of others. It is a bathing of the whole soul in love and acceptance.

And this brings us to Step Six.

STEP 6

Accept Yourself and Others As You Are

Acceptance is a funny thing. On the one hand, we're saying accept your mistakes and learn from them. On the other hand we're saying you are okay just as you are.

We're saying: accept your darkness and bring it to the light. When you bring it to the light, the darkness will disappear. But what if it doesn't?

Sometimes when I try to bring my darkness to the light, it's the light that seems to disappear, and I'm left sitting in deeper darkness. What do I do then?

Then I have a simple choice, I can beat myself, feel like a failure and condemn God and the world, or I can accept where I am. "Here I am in the darkness and there doesn't seem to be any light. That's okay. This is just where I am. No praise. No blame."

When I do that, I become the light I was looking for. Every gesture of self-acceptance unveils the inner light and helps to light my way. It may only do so two feet ahead of me, but that's okay. When I accept myself, the next step comes by itself.

God's love, grace, guidance, whatever you might call it, comes through the channel of your love for yourself. When you accept yourself as you are, you open that channel. The same thing happens when you accept others as they are.

The way to peace is a simple one, if you are willing to practice it:

1. Accept yourself as you are. You are okay with all of your problems, pains, and preoccupations. You don't have to change anything. You don't have to obtain anything or get rid of anything. You are perfect right here and now. Let that knowledge in. As you do, the judgments fall away by themselves.

2. Accept others as they are. They are okay with all their apparent assets and liabilities. You don't have to change them. They don't need to improve themselves to deserve your acceptance. They don't need your approval and you don't need theirs. They are okay and you are okay. Nobody is right. Nobody is wrong. You exist side by side. As you accept others, your heart opens. As you accept others, you become more gentle with yourself.

3. Accept your life as it is right now. You don't have to change anything about it. Every situation is perfect as it is. Every relationship is perfect as it is. Every lesson enables you to grow. Every outer obstacle helps you turn deeper within to the very Source of love. Don't interpret your life or you will find that something is missing. Nothing is missing. Your interpretations for or against are the illusion you are here to break through. Accept your life just as it is. Then,

every belief that does not honor you or does not honor others will fall away, because there is nothing to support it. Into the empty space you make in your heart through your refusal to judge, love's presence flows. Now you are not alone. Now your companion has arrived.

Acceptance is such a simple thing, yet it is the hardest thing we learn to do. For with acceptance, our ego steps aside. With acceptance, the barriers to love's presence dissolve.

This path is the path of acceptance. What you can't accept you will oppose, and in that opposition will be your bondage. What you accept, moves gently through your heart. Nothing pushes you. Nothing holds you back. You move wherever love would have you go.

This is a moment to moment proposition. In each moment, resistance or attachment comes. We watch it come. We watch the struggle. We watch ourselves grow tired until at last we let go. We let the struggle play itself out. It always does.

We become more patient. More forgiving. More relaxed. We learn to be gentle with ourselves and others.

It doesn't seem to be such a victory, but it is. When nothing stands between us and our peace, even if just for a moment, we experience divinity inside and out. There is no separation.

This is the fruit of the path of acceptance.

Remember, there is never a moment in our experience when acceptance of ourselves and our brothers and sisters will not restore our peace. There is never a moment when there are no obstacles to surrender.

We accept this not as a goal, but as a practice. For in the practice, the goal is met.

STEP 7

Be Willing to Learn and Share

As soon as I think I've got it all figured out, my love supply leaves me. Why is this?

Because I shut the door in my head. And I shut the door in my heart. I say "Enough. I've had enough."

Well apparently my inner teacher does not agree. And I have yet another lesson to learn in humility.

Everything I know means nothing if in this moment I am not at peace. And when I am at peace, the need to know falls away.

A Course in Miracles says that we teach what we need to learn. That is an important awareness. When I stand up to share my experiences with you I am reinforcing my learning process.

By sharing, I deepen what I have learned. I extend it through the chakras. I take an intellectual knowledge, personalize it and move it into the heart. When you hear me deeply, I know that what is true for me is also true for you.

By sharing, I learn to listen to you. I see how you have internalized in a different way, with a different emphasis. It becomes clear that certain lessons I am still muddling through you have mastered. I understand that you are my teacher as much as I am yours.

Teaching and learning are lifelong processes. Even when I am playing the role of teacher, I am learning and even when I am playing the role of learner, I am teaching.

How I learn becomes a teaching. And how I teach becomes a learning. You see, it goes on and on. There is never a point in my life when I cannot benefit from the feedback you give me. Even if 99% of it is judgment of me, I can still savor the 1% that is true.

Not only must teachers take responsibility for what they teach by learning it themselves, but learners must also take responsibility for what they learn. Nobody teaches you something without your permission.

So I am always learning. And so are you. That is the basis on which we meet, face to face, as equals.

While I can do some of my spiritual work alone through meditating, witnessing my thoughts and feelings, and studying scriptures, there is a major piece that I cannot do alone.

I can't overcome projection unless I experience it. I need to project onto you and I need you to project onto me so I can experience this phenomenon. I need to experience my apparent separation from you before I can reject that separateness as an illusion.

None of us are saved alone. It is through our interactions, as painful as they are, that we learn and grow.

So if I isolate myself from others, I am just postponing my atonement. Sooner or later, you and I must meet and play out our drama.

Without interaction, our two separate selves would never understand God's love. The need for interaction is confirmed by the fact that one part of God's creation feels separate from another. Wherever separation is felt, interaction is necessary as a bridge.

This is true, even if we spend all our time beating up on each other. The problem is that then we get divorced and go our separate ways thinking "Oh well, it didn't work," and look for someone else to be cozy with.

We keep trying to join together and we keep failing, because that is not what is being asked of us. God does not ask us to join. S/He asks us to honor one another.

The golden rule says: "Do unto others as you would have them do unto you." It doesn't say: "merge into one cozy person."

As long as we keep trying to merge, we will keep missing the point. We are not here to find our salvation "in each other" but "through each other."

Joining with each other is not necessary because we are already joined in Spirit. In our ego-based reality, we appear to be separate. We appear to have different personalities and different needs. We keep trying to join at that level, but we can't. Joining takes place when those differences fall away.

When we "do unto others as we would have them do unto us" we emphasize the only thing we rightfully share as separate beings: our equality. In honoring each other as equals, we assume correct relationship to each other and enable the divine presence to manifest through us. As Martin Buber says, God does not exist "in you" or "in me" but "where we meet."

Finding "where we meet" is the dance of life. It is also one of our primary spiritual practices.

Every opportunity we take to share our thoughts and feelings with others helps us reach beyond our ego-based reality to discover our common aspirations and needs. Every time we open our hearts to each other, we actively dissolve the illusion of separation between us.

In the final analysis, we do not come together "to join" but to witness that we are already joined, heart to heart and mind to mind. We can step out of that joining by judging and emphasizing our differences, or we can remain together by accepting and blessing every person just as he or she is.

The more we come to the shared space, the sacred circle, the more we realize that it is home, and that every ego excursion is a detour. That doesn't mean that we stop going away, but that even while we are moving away from each other, we are looking forward to coming back together.

We know where home is. And we know that we can return when we are ready.

STEP 8

Be Your Own Authority

L et's be clear. Being your own authority does not mean being an authority for anyone else! It just means that you don't let any one else become an authority for you.

Everyone is free to choose, including you. And everyone is responsible for the choice that he or she makes. How else could it be?

Many people try to cross these clear lines of responsibility, but doing so only clouds their perception of reality. Don't be a glutton for punishment. Honor these lines and you will honor each other.

First, understand that you are not taking responsibility for yourself when:

1. You let someone else make choices for you, or

2. You make choices for someone else.

That is co-dependence. It is not empowering to yourself or

the other person. It may appear to gain you a temporary advantage, but you pay for that advantage by forfeiting your freedom to choose your own life.

It's great to listen to others and learn from others. Intimate sharing is essential to your spiritual growth. It gives you feedback that you can use to expand your perceptions. But others do not know what you need. Even psychics and other intuitive persons cannot tell you what you need to know. They may supply an important piece of information or they may not. Either way, you are the person who must use this information to find your peace.

Understand that there are limits on what anyone can tell you that will be truly helpful. Those limits apply to what you can tell others. The most help you can give or receive from others is encouragement. Anything more than that is rarely helpful.

To be your own authority, you must let go of the concept that there is an answer outside of you. You must let go of the concept that there is something to achieve.

Authority comes directly out of experience. It says: "I honor my life. I accept what is true for me, even if it is not true for others."

Inner authority is inconsistent with prescribing for others. As soon as you try to make others fit with your values and beliefs, you undercut the power of those values and beliefs in your own life. As soon as you need the agreement of others to honor your own life, you have lost touch with your inner authority.

Everyone has the right, indeed the responsibility to say "This is true for me. This works for me." This is an important self-affirmation. For nobody's life is exactly like mine. My experiences are unique, and should be accepted as such.

Anyone who attempts to deny me the integrity of my experience denies his or her own experience as well. It is impossible to affirm oneself by denying others.

So all of my energy that is invested in denial and judgment of others keeps me from my guidance and my truth. I don't begin to know what is true for me until I honor the experience of others.

Conversely, I don't begin to hear my own truth as long as I am more invested in the experience of others than I am in my own experience. Authority comes from within and stops at the skin.

My authority sets boundaries on my desire to choose when that desire infringes on the freedom and responsibility of others to choose for themselves. It also empowers me to choose for myself when others would make choices for me.

My authority is consistent with and equal to your authority. You cannot deny or overstep your authority without inviting me to do the same. In that sense, your fidelity to your own experience supports your innocence as well as mine.

Now, all of this said, it is clear that overstepping and understepping our authority is part of our learning process here. It is part of our dance with each other.

Thus, it must not be our intention to end the dance, but to witness it. Witnessing the dance brings the movements in toward the center. It makes them more visible. As we become aware of our "over-" and "under-stepping," correction happens naturally. Witnessing helps us see and learn from our own behavior without judging it.

The authority issue is one of the most profound issues we will ever deal with. There is not one of us who will not puff himself up and beat himself into the ground. We do not learn our existential authority until we see the falsehood of our ego-based authority. The one comes from simple acceptance of ourselves and others. The other comes from a deep sense of inadequacy which we project onto others.

Those who have illusions of superiority over others often harbor unconscious feelings of inferiority. And those who consistently defer to the strength or wisdom of others often harbor unconscious feelings of superiority. Strangely enough, neither the person playing the superior role nor the person playing the inferior role has the willingness to stand alone with his or her convictions. In one way or another, both seek the support and agreement of others.

We must wake up to the fact that we can be too strong or too weak for our own good. Those who study the *I Ching* will not find this concept difficult. Those who are too strong attract the weak and so become weak themselves. And those who are too weak attract the strong, and so become stronger through them.

Each uses the other to come to balance. Unfortunately this is not a conscious process, and so there is little understanding or gratitude for the exchange.

It seems important at this stage of our collective evolution that this process of "coming to balance" be a conscious one. That is why there is so much literature coming out on abuse and co-dependency. These exchanges, when they happen unconsciously, leave many unspeakable wounds.

Speaking about our wounds is healthy. It is our way of "owning" our experience and taking responsibility for our healing.

All this is about RESPECT, respect for ourselves and respect for others. Respect comes from the word "specere" which means to look. Re-spect therefore means "to look back, to see again, or to see differently."

It is understood that first we will "see through glass darkly, and then face to face." First we will misperceive and then our perception will be corrected. First we will make mistakes and then we will learn. First, we will trespass against one another, and then we will forgive.

This is a process repeated again and again. Respect for ourselves and others is something we gain by violating the law of equality. The awareness of our violation in and of itself draws us toward equality.

So when we say "Be Your Own Authority" what we mean is learn to be who you truly are and learn to see others as they truly are. Practice equality. Learn from inequality. Accept the process. Use it to align and to grow.

THIRD CORNERSTONE

Trusting Your Life

Much of our life takes us to the edge of our boundaries and leaves us there. It says: "You are not limited to what is inside of these boundaries."

As if to confirm that insight, we see ourselves hitting up against every boundary we create. Every time we take a stand — it almost does not matter what stance we take — we separate a unified reality into two apparent parts. Call those parts whatever you like: good and bad, male and female, high and low.

Out of unity, we make duality. As soon as I say "I," I get you, which means "not-I." Even if I say "we," I mean "not them."

No matter how much I expand my consciousness, I continue to encounter people or situations which I cannot accept. There, I draw the line. I establish my boundaries. What is on this side of the line is acceptable. And what is on that side of the line is not.

This is the nature of my journey of consciousness. My whole life is a process of establishing and erasing boundaries. When I can see it that way, I learn to be lighter with myself and others. I know the boundaries are not real. My beliefs just make them seem real. When I change my beliefs, those boundaries just disappear.

I am always trying to define and order my existence. The harder I try, the more I make a botch of things. I'm just not very good at controlling my life. Sooner or later, I come to that conclusion.

Sooner or later, I realize that my purpose here is not to try to control my life. It is to work with it.

I can say what I want. There is nothing wrong with that. But I must choose what I get, whether or not it is what I want.

Often, I believe what happens isn't what I wanted. But, later, I find that it is exactly what I needed at the time. Sooner or later, I come to realize that I don't know what I need.

But my life force does. My life force knows what I need and attracts it to me. I used to call my life force "fate" or "God," but that never worked because it put it outside of me.

It isn't! It isn't outside or inside, or maybe it's both. When I draw the line, it retreats so deep inside I can't find it or it expands beyond all the limits I imagine. It is so small it is completely incognito. Look for it in the body/mind and you cannot find it.

How much does the brain weigh? It is lighter than that. How much does the soul weigh? It is lighter even than that! Too light to be weighed, it is beyond gravity. Yet it is so extensive even the universe is not big enough to contain it!

When I look at who I really am, I see no limits, no inside, no outside. When I look at who I really am, I am no different from you. I am no different from God. It is all the same. It's all one movement of life force without beginning or end!

When I'm inside my boundaries, everything seems so important. When life comes in and erases those boundaries, I realize all those things I thought so important were insignificant.

Each wave is a purification, a dissolution of attachments, a wiping clean of the slate of judgment and evaluation. As my friend Jim said after a recent conference, "I was so blissed out, I couldn't fill out the evaluation form!"

Slowly the swirling energies of my life slow down to a gentle dance. It is extraordinary! I begin to find that my life is okay just as it is. I don't have to change anything about it. I don't have to change my relationships, or my job, or where I live to be happy. I am happy here, right now, as I am. Life has come to me and I have embraced it, simply and profoundly.

I do not know what the next moment will bring, but it does not matter. Whatever comes will be fine. For I left fear behind with my judgments. No stain of the past clings to my innocence; no expectation of the future shrouds my freedom to be myself or to let you be. I dwell simply with the understanding that I am okay as I am, and you are okay as you are, and life is fine just as it is. That is my bliss. That is my substance.

The rest is just size and shape. The rest is just form that returns to dust whence it came.

The insubstantial cannot contain the substantial. Boundaries cannot contain the formless. The limited mind cannot contain the mind of God.

But the mind of God contains all things. It is a cup that is forever empty. No matter how much wine we pour into it, it never gets filled up. That is the profound blessing we are all coming to. That is the prayer on our lips, the forgotten song we remember as our hearts open to each other. It simply says. "Welcome, brother and sister. The place you left has remained empty, awaiting your return. Welcome home."

STEP 9

Accept the Lesson

Life never brings me what I expect. If it did, I wouldn't learn anything. Inevitably, my expectations must be disappointed, so that I can reach out to a deeper and wider reality.

Every lesson that comes to me seeks to awaken, not to punish me. As long as I think that God or the universe is trying to punish me, I will be unable to accept my lesson and learn from it.

In truth, each lesson seeks to lift me up. If I am propped up, it may dethrone me before it inspires me, but its goal is always to uplift.

Of course, my lesson and my interpretation of the lesson are always 180 degrees apart! I simply cannot understand my lesson at the ego level. The lesson always takes me beyond ego.

If I am looking for ego-reinforcement, I will not get it from God. Yet I make my faith in God contingent on getting sufficient ego reinforcement!

No wonder I get frustrated! As soon as I think I am free of my old conceptual limitations, I get yanked back into the fray.

Learning my lessons takes a great deal of compassion for myself. I need to realize that it isn't easy for me to change how I perceive reality. If it was, I wouldn't need a lesson to practice it.

So I need to be patient. I need to go at my own pace. There is no hurry. Most of my lessons are not achievement-oriented. They are perception-oriented. I don't need to change myself, change others, or change the world. I need to change my perceptions of self, other, and the world.

I misunderstand my lessons if I think they ask me to be something I am not or give something I don't have to give. If fear comes up, they ask me to walk through it. If something is a burden to me, they ask me to lay it down.

Whatever the lesson, it is perfect for me. It asks me to make exactly the adjustment that I am able to make. It never asks for more than I can give.

So trust becomes a factor. The more I trust my lessons, the more I cooperate with them and the better I learn them.

Instead of being suspicious of the unknown, I welcome it. I see how it expands me and makes a deeper place for love to dwell.

Obviously, this is not as easy as it sounds. When I have pain in my life, I automatically tense up. I resist the pain. I fight the pain. I complain about the pain. Rarely, do I accept the pain and ask what message it brings. My tendency to resist pain comes from my belief that pain is an attack against me. So I try to exorcise it. But that just deepens the pain. Through experience, I learn that the way out of pain is not through resistance, but through acceptance.

It is an awesome paradox. The only way the pain dissolves is when I am no longer invested in its going away. As long a I am trying to get rid of it, the pain persists.

The pain is not a punishment, but a communication. It tells me that something is awry. It asks me to make some kind of adjustment. It asks me to come to a new awareness.

In the same manner, every lesson asks me to open my heart and mind in a new way. Old defense mechanisms that are no longer needed for my survival must be surrendered. Inch by inch the territory claimed by fear must open to love's embrace.

It is a gradual process. I am not asked to open up all at once. As long as I'm making progress, I am cooperating with my lesson .

That does not mean that I do not encounter resistance. I do periodically. My goal should not be to try to get rid of resistance but to notice when it comes and when it goes. That way I begin to understand how my thoughts, feelings and beliefs influence my life.

More and more I realize that it is not what happens in my life that matters, but how I react to what happens. By placing emphasis on my reactions, which I can influence, I empower myself to deal creatively with the many challenging situations that life presents me.

I am no longer a victim of unsavory forces outside of me, but a protagonist, positively influencing the outcome of events by maintaining an attitude of trust, hope and faith. Indeed, whenever something happens that disturbs my peace, I realize that my attitude toward life has taken a nose dive. When I take the time to look within and lift up my heart, I see a more graceful and cooperative world around me.

Contrary to our old programming, the events in our lives are never fixed. And they never mean what we think they do. Everything is in motion, including our thoughts and feelings. Thus, if we really want to understand what is happening in our lives, we need to "be with" the situation for a while. Once I have taken the time to sense what is happening, I have a better chance of responding to it appropriately.

The worst thing we can do with a lesson is to decide what it means right away. We need to be with the situation without judging or interpreting it. We need to feel it, get a sense of it, see how it moves as our thoughts and feelings change.

This is a process of listening within. Eugene Gendelin wrote a book called *Focusing* that provides a helpful step by step technique for tuning in to our deep feeling sensibility. Meditation techniques are also helpful.

When we sit with a problem situation, we don't try to analyze it or figure it out intellectually. Doing that is trying to address the problem from the same level on which it exists. It doesn't work. We need to sink down into the body and ground ourselves. We need to move out of our "thinking mind" into our "feeling mind."

The Feeling Mind contains the whole situation. It does not select one piece at another's expense. It does not seek to choose, for choice would only aggravate the conflict. It just reaches out to contain all the aspects, all the polarities, all the contradictions. It embraces the situation as a whole, without judging it. It just lets everything be fully present in consciousness.

That act of letting it all be enables a subtle shift to occur in consciousness. In that shift, the goal becomes not "to solve the problem" or to "choose" between polarized positions, but to bridge those positions by changing the perception that they are mutually exclusive.

This is similar to negotiating between two people who disagree. Often, a third person is essential when two people want to work out their issues. This person — be it an arbitrator or therapist — is charged with finding the common ground where both people can be heard and have their needs addressed.

The mediator shifts the agenda from "either/or" to "both together." The mediator helps to build a "we" consciousness in both people. It is in this "we" space that problems are solved. Indeed, in the "we" space, the problem no longer exists. It was only a problem because it was seen by each party from an ego space.

The same thing is true in consciousness itself. Problems are not solved from narrow ego-perceptions which are conflict ridden, but from the expanded vision of spirit, in which all contradictions can be contained.

Sitting with a problem then involves a change in consciousness, a movement from the "thinking mind" to the "feeling mind." It also involves a movement from a mindscape in which the contents of consciousness are seen as polarized and opposed to each other to a mindscape in which they are seen as co-existing and contained.

The establishment of peace within the mind, peace between individuals, and peace among nations involves the same principles. In every case, it involves a change in intention and attention, a change in consciousness and perception.

When I am fighting my lesson, it is my enemy. When I am

accepting it, it is my friend. I always establish my relationship toward my lesson and the relationship I establish determines whether I resist that lesson, or learn it and move on.

A teaching that does not allow for lessons to be learned is not a spiritual teaching, but a form of indoctrination. Lessons are always learned by opening the heart and opening the mind. They have nothing to do with rigid concepts and moral absolutes. They are always experiential.

So our lives are laboratories for learning. Our mental and emotional experience is a classroom in which we learn to blame or to bless, to reject or accept, to control or to set free.

STEP 10

See That Everything Is Okay As It Is

When *A Course in Miracles* asks us to "Choose Again," it invites us to change our perception, to see things differently. It asks us to recognize inequality and choose equality. It asks us to recognize our fear and understand that love is what we want.

And if we can't change our perception, and if we can't see that it is love that we want, then it asks us merely to be aware that we can't. Awareness is always enough. This whole experience is about expanding our awareness.

So long as I am aware that I have a choice, it does not matter that I am unable to choose love. Can you embrace that?

The ego wants to say: "You filthy person. You screwed up again. You forgot to choose love. You're never going to get this stuff."

And we all know that this voice will surface. But behind this voice is another one that says "It's okay. Don't worry about it. Just be aware. You did fine."

We know that this is Spirit's voice because it honors us, and it honors everyone else in our drama too. It does not build us up at the expense of others, nor does it drag us down to lift up others. It says: "It's okay. You judged. He took offense and attacked. You attacked back. Now you both feel terrible. Just be aware of what happened. No judgment is necessary."

According to Spirit, I don't have to be right all the time to be acceptable. I am acceptable even when I make mistakes. I am acceptable even when I make the same mistake twice or three times. And so is my brother or sister.

There's one standard for all of us and that standard is: "mistakes are part of the learning process and so is forgiveness." Judgment and blame are false interpretations not only of what happened but what it is for.

Everything that happens in our lives has but one intention: to remove "the blocks to love's presence;" to dissolve "the obstacles to peace." Every struggle, every knock-down drag out fight is but a tool to awaken, a reminder to choose again.

Whenever we feel outrage, whenever we feel that we are being unjustly punished or taken advantage of, we need to remember this. There is always something to learn, something to release, something to be grateful for.

How can love be an attack? If the basic state of creation is a state of love, then even when we feel attacked love is present. Even in the midst of our suffering, peace is possible.

Every moment we live is a moment that asks us to make some gesture of forgiveness. Every time we judge ourselves or another, every time we feel fear and attack, every time we want to attack but force ourselves not to, every time we justify our attack or our defense, we are asked to forgive. But what does this mean?

It means that I realize first of all that however I feel is just how I feel now. I may have felt that way in the past, but that doesn't make this any more real than that was.

Using the past to justify my anger, just reinforces my anger. So I must leave the past be.

I don't carry the past into the present and I don't carry the present into the future. I just accept the present as it is. That is forgiveness.

It is not something esoteric. I just let whatever is "be." I don't struggle with it. I don't try to change it. I just let it be. I allow it to be with me and I allow myself to be with it.

I'm like a winemaker. My experience is the wine. I put it into the cask of acceptance and let it age. In time, acceptance ripens into understanding. In time, my experience becomes a living truth that guides me and inspires others.

This requires a lot of patience. It means I have to acknowledge that the wine will be much better when it has aged. If I drink it too soon, before I have lived with it, my experience cannot teach me. It just reinforces what I have learned in the past, much of which may no longer be relevant.

I need to recognize that change is not bad. It is a ripening process. If I did not change, I would not ripen. If I did not stay with my experience, I would not learn from it.

As long as I am invested in keeping everything the same, I cannot benefit from the lessons that my life spontaneously provides me. I must be willing to change. But I must not be so proud as to think I know the direction in which change is required.

That I do not know. That I should not know. That comes from the unknown, from beyond me, or from so deep within me I do not recognize it. It comes through me and transforms me as it passes through.

Knowing that everything is okay is simply trusting the process, whatever it brings. It means that I know that my Creator loves me and abides with me through all my travails. She cannot interfere with my lessons, for She did not prescribe them.

She is simply my witness as I am Hers. Nothing less, nothing more.

STEP 11

Look in the Mirror

No matter where we turn, we see our own shadow. Sometimes it looks back toward us through the faces of our brothers. Sometimes it skips before us as we run full tilt in the wind.

Our shadows do not disappear. They remain with us.

Everything we are afraid of is personified somehow. Yet it belongs to us. Everything we see on the outside of the body/mind confirms an inside reality.

If you take that inner reality without outside reflection, what you have is the death state, a state empty of projection, a state in which interaction is unnecessary, because the parts of the whole are no longer separate.

But in this world, there is an inside and an outside. There is an image and a reflection.

There is a mind that thinks and a mind that feels. The feeling mind reflects the thinking mind, because every feeling is a reflection of a thought. Often, it is hard to separate the feeling from the thought, so closely does one follow from the other.

The whole psyche is a field or array of thinking and feeling states intricately bound together. Each field of consciousness intersects and interacts with others, further complicating the picture. Indeed, it is impossible to grasp the component parts or the number of relationships between them.

What we can grasp, however, is that at any moment in time what we see outside of us reflects our internal field of consciousness, or unique array of thought/feeling constructs. As such it is a mirror for us. Looking in this mirror can be painful, but it is not nearly so painful as pretending that the mirror is not there.

Every person who walks into our lives and pushes our buttons is but a personification of our own shadow. They have no objective significance in our lives. Often we return the favor, pushing their buttons too. Our interaction is totally subjective. It is the relationship of one shadow to another.

Only when one person wakes up and understands that the interaction is all about his own shadow — what he hates, cannot accept, or fears about himself — does the mirroring stop. That awareness removes the hook, destroys the projection. Interactions like this cannot continue except through the agreement (usually unconscious) of both parties.

We don't look into the mirror to learn to hate ourselves, but to recognize our repressed judgments. These judgments sabotage our ability to feel whole in ourselves or in relationship with others. Thus, the descent into the darkness of our own psyche is essential to our healing process. Without the descent, we cannot become light-bearers.

Interestingly, this descent into the darkness and subsequent ascent into the light does not happen in a linear manner. It is a cyclical journey. First I face some previously denied fear, bring it to the light, and then another one surfaces. Sound familiar? Each victory is followed by a subsequent challenge.

We have done ourselves a disservice by looking at our spiritual processes through the eyes of the world or the ego. From the perspective of both the ego and the world, we are all miserable failures. Linear, step by step, task-oriented thinking simply cannot penetrate to the meaning of cyclical processes. Only the intuitive, feeling mind understands the concepts of polarity and change.

Collectively, eastern traditions are more comfortable with the feeling mind. Indeed, the Taoist tradition, from which comes the *I Ching*, the *Tao Te Ching* and other masterpieces of spiritual understanding, offers us some of the deepest insights into the process of change.

To the Taoists, everything is energy in motion. Even ideas that seem to have reached their apex or nadir recycle by moving toward the opposite pole. To the eastern mind, life is a pendulum, moving back and forth; it is not a linear journey in one direction.

This perspective helps us understand that our spiritual progress is not to be measured by how many lessons we receive, or even by how many of them we learn, but by our willingness to look in the mirror when it is handed to us. *A Course in Miracles* says that this "little willingness" is enough.

In that respect, every time we are willing, we move to encompass all of our lessons simultaneously. Every time we open our hearts, we have a taste of what it feels like to be truly open.

So every lesson is a widening and deepening of consciousness. It is a stretching of the mind beyond its conceptual limits and a stretching of the heart beyond its emotional boundaries. It is a bringing of unconscious material into consciousness, a healing of past wounds, and a discovery of a new faith and trust.

One success brings another challenge. One failure brings an opportunity to choose again. There is absolutely no judgment implied in this.

Subjective processes don't have a beginning or an end in time. That is hard for us to understand and accept. But it's an essential awareness if we are to look into the mirror over and over again without getting dispirited or depressed. After enough mirror gazing, we all develop our "cosmic sense of humor." We no longer try to be perfect, or try to get all our work done in time. We become content with whatever life brings. Just to deal with what comes up without crucifying ourselves or others is enough of a challenge.

And we're smart enough, or experienced enough, to know that every once in a while we are going to blow it. I mean, we're going to completely forget everything we ever learned and do the most stupid thing we can imagine. All our worst fears are going to come true. We're going to be embarrassed, outraged, turned inside out. And, somehow, we're going to survive that. And perhaps even see it as a gift.

And then, we really know that the journey goes round and round. And we know that we're okay, regardless of where we seem to be or what seems to be happening. And this brings us to the last step, which we must know by now, is also the first.

STEP 12

Open Your Heart

The easiest way to open your heart is to ask for help or to offer it. If you are having difficulty, ask for help. Ask a friend. Ask a stranger. Ask God. Ask.

The door in your heart cannot open if you do not give it permission to open. Asking is giving permission. It is an invitation to the Holy Spirit to help you see things differently. It is an invitation to your brothers and sisters to shower you with love and acceptance.

"Ask and it shall be opened." Your heartfelt request is always answered. The answer may not appear in the form you expect, but it is there if you are willing to look. The very act of looking opens you to finding it.

Are you looking for love? Then you will find it. If it doesn't appear right away, keep looking. If love doesn't meet your expectations, throw them away. Love is there, somewhere. Change every idea or perception that blocks your awareness of love's presence and you will surely find it.

Remember, if you are not looking for love, you aren't going to find it. So don't be shy.

If you want to open your heart, offer to be of help to someone. Approach a friend or a stranger; it doesn't matter. Let your intuition guide you. Somewhere out there, someone is calling out for love. No, not obviously. But silently. And you will know who it is.

Offer love without strings attached. Offer to help without expecting anything in return. That will open your heart. And it will open the hearts of others.

Each one of us holds the key to salvation. And we can offer it to each other with a gesture of support, a gentle word of encouragement. We can offer it to each other by seeing every attack as a call for love.

The heart opens when we accept ourselves with all our contradictions, all our liabilities, all our struggles. The heart opens when we accept another person with all their trials and tribulations. The heart opens when we offer love simply, as we would to a hurt child. And it opens when the hurt child within reaches out for the love that is offered to him.

There is nothing mysterious about what opens the heart. Acceptance does.

There is nothing mysterious about what closes the heart. Judgment does.

The heart is a spiritual muscle. It opens and closes. The more it works the stronger it gets.

Don't judge yourself if you feel your heart tighten. It does so merely to open again. All you need do is allow it.

Let the pain come and go. Let everything pass through you. Breathe deeply. Let the air come in and out. Be a channel for life. Don't resist on the inhale or hold onto the exhale. Just let the breath come and go.

Just let life come and go, with its ups and downs. Don't be attached to either. Don't be afraid of either.

No matter how hard you try, you are not going to change the ebb and flow of life. It continues regardless of whether you hold on or let go.

When you hold on, the muscles tighten. When you let go, they release. Are you tight now? It's okay. Just be aware of it. In the awareness itself is the release.

To open your heart, you must be willing to move with the ebb and the flow, the contraction and the release. Don't expect to ride the peaks without descending to the troughs.

To open your heart, you must be willing to be present with whatever is happening here and now. You do not have "to do" anything. You just need "to be." That is enough.

Be with yourself. Be with others. Be with God. That is enough.

Acrobatics are nice to watch, but they are not necessary. You don't have to jump through hoops for love. You just need to be willing to receive it. You just need to be willing to give it.

You do not decide where love comes from or where it goes. It just comes and you let it in. It just comes in and you let it go. Consciousness is a channel for love, not its origin.

The more you become a conduit for love, the more you realize this. Love is the only power. Everything apart from love is but a container for it.

Love is real. The body/mind is just a conduit. Its reality is to be found in its fulfillment of its purpose.

By itself the body/mind is just a bundle of worries and fears, expectations and judgments. It is a temporary, self-destructive phenomenon. It is born. It suffers. And it dies. It has no purpose by itself.

Its only purpose is as a container for love. It is love's body, love's mind, love's speech, love's action. It is love sitting silently and love dancing.

As we open through our self acceptance and acceptance of others, we begin to see this. As we ask for help and offer it, we begin to understand that our bodies and minds are containers for an unbelievably powerful energy. This energy cannot be manipulated or controlled. But it can be experienced.

There comes a time in our spiritual development when we understand the concepts well enough. We don't need to read any more books or go to any more workshops. We just need to apply what we already know in our daily lives.

In a very profound sense, this is the moment when we make a commitment to our spiritual path. All that happened to this point was just preparation for this moment of surrender. This is the baptism by fire of which Jesus spoke. This is the moment when we are born again in spirit.

Now each day becomes a living teaching for us. The need for special teachers and special books falls away. Every brother or sister is a teacher. Every event in our lives is an unfolding of profound scripture.

Our friends look aghast as we make a bonfire and throw our spiritual books into the flames.

The outer husk falls away. The inside kernel blooms. Actions speak louder than words.

We all come to this place where we fall simply and beauti-fully into the heart. And we know that it is no longer what we say that matters, but how we say it. And it doesn't matter what we do, but how we do it. We know that all of our beliefs mean absolutely nothing if we do not see, and speak and act through the eyes, and lips and lineaments of love.

This is a place we come to not just once, but many times. At first, we are uncomfortable here, and rush back into the safety of our concepts and goals. Subsequently, we are able to be here for a while and recharge emotionally. Before long, we yearn for this place where we can be without struggle. And when we arrive, we do not want to leave.

That's okay. Home is not a place where we live all the time. It is a place from which we go out and to which we return, again and again.

Home is here where we can be together without discomfort or unnecessary words. Welcome brother. Welcome sister. I greet you as you come in. I salute you as you go out.

May you be well. May your life bring you many blessings.

FOURTH CORNERSTONE

Remembering God's Love

There are always events and circumstances which come up in life which stun us, knock us off our feet, pull us out of our comfort zone. We lose a job, or someone dies, or a relationship ends. And we feel attacked, disappointed, let down. We feel that we have failed.

Every seemingly negative event in our lives plays first to our guilt. And before we know it, we have sunk into an emotional black hole. There, we are not worthy. God does not love us. Others do not care about us. And our lives are empty and without meaning.

Who has not been in this place?

This is not just the place of unmet expectations, but the place of existential grief, the place outside the garden, where tears flow long and deep in the shadow of what could have been. This is the place of old collective wounds.

We do not know it, but it is our intimacy with the divine we mourn. Our connection to our Mother/Father has become tenuous and torn. Our feelings of separation intensify the more we try to run our lives. Our fragmentation increases as long as we focus on the part of our lives that seems empty.

From our aloneness, we cry out, not expecting to be heard. Yet it is precisely in this place of woundedness and awkward silence that our Mother/Father addresses us. We have come emptied out, ready to listen. We have come humbled and reaching out. We have come hoping against hope. We have come knowing there must be something here, but without knowing what it is.

If you have not been in this place, I cannot describe it to you. If you have been in this place, and not felt something stirring inside, some warmth and rustle of wings through the pain, then I cannot help you.

This is a place each of us must encounter alone. This is the room, from which no one leaves without being transformed.

From the place of brokenness, wings are mended. Old pains are purged. Guilt is emptied from its bottomless cup. Darkness is taken into midnight toward dawn. The stain of blood from the wound sealed in the heart can be seen on the skin. A body appears on the empty cross.

A man or woman comes to this earth not to suffer, but to let suffering go. Some think this can be done through denial. They must find out that it is not possible.

The route to joy goes through suffering. On it one stumbles unexpectedly on the only tool the journey offers. At first, one does not even understand that it is a tool.

In my pain, I find forgiveness. In my pain, I find God's love. It does not happen until I allow it. It may take a very long time. But when I reach out, I see that release is possible. When I open my heart to the unseen presence, I feel it join with me. I feel it help me to my feet. It feel it stand and walk with me and guide my journey.

Some never find the tool. They withhold from others what they must learn to give to themselves. And they withhold from themselves what they must learn to give to others. They turn to face the mirror without recognizing the image that looks back at them. They break the glass and use it to cut their way free.

But freedom cannot be won with claws. Every claw has a wing, dimly remembered, a wing that waits to be tested in the solitude of the heart. Every soul has an appointment with God.

From the moment that meeting takes place, we know at last that we are not alone. We know that all of the pain, all of the separation, all of the guilt and the shame is an illusion. We know that we are loved and that there was never a time when we were not loved.

Then we move away from the intensity of that moment. Our lives become more predictable again. Our sight narrows. Our reach pulls in. Our attention wanders. We are restless. We are bored. We need to cook up a new crisis. We need to climb out on a limb so that we can crash to the ground again.

We do not have to play out this charade. But we do. Our "little willingness" is attached to our pain. Without our pain, we can not surrender. Without our pain, we cannot remember that it is impossible for us to control anything in life. Without being touched deep down within, we still believe that we are in charge and that we know what we are doing.

Nothing, of course, could be further from the truth. That is the lesson of all our pain and suffering. That is the lesson of the illusion. We seem to be in control, but we're not. We think we know what we need, but we don't.

Every thing we strive for, everything we perceive, is full of the emptiness we bring to it. We search for fullness, but never find it, because it does not exist apart from ourselves. And it is not part of the ego-mentality. It is not part of the search and the laws of the search. It does not obey the laws of emptiness.

Do you begin to understand? Every loss, every pain, brings us to the empty place within where God abides and waits for us. If we would fill it up, S/he will always defer. Any and every addiction, expectation, or belief system interposes between God and us, and claims the place of silence. If we would be with God, we must go empty-handed, without thought to the place where we may listen and dwell. This, in time, we come to understand. This, we come to grasp, is not an outer place, but a place within.

It is not a meditation room or a church, but an instant in time, hallowed by our intention. It opens when we allow it, when we are upset and ask for help. When we are dislodged from our routine, cast out, upturned, and ready for help, the temple is ready.

In the moment of our emotional upheaval, when we have lost peace, for whatever reason, we need but leave everything behind and enter. We need but leave behind the thoughts that would judge, the temptation to evaluate or give meaning to what we see. We need but leave behind what we perceive and enter.

For "nothing we see means anything. We have given everything all the meaning it has for us." We think we know what it is, but we don't. We think we know who we are, but we don't. We don't know anything. We don't know. Naked, we enter the heart. Empty-handed and without thought, we enter the place of silences.

Living in the consciousness of God's love means coming to grips with our utter powerlessness to understand anything on our own. It means surrendering our need to know or control. It means learning to trust that everything that happens has a reason, though it can't be seen. Everything that enters my life brings a silent blessing, though I may not be able to feel it.

When I am wounded, let me remember God's love. Let me not evaluate or judge, or think I know why. Let me not attack or defend, deny or justify. Let me just remember God's love.

That is all I need. That is all there is.

In place of the illusion, let me find this simple truth. Before the power of God's love in me, everything else pales. All that I hope for is insignificant in the face of this all pervading love that moves through me and you and everyone who opens to it.

In the place of games of power, let me surrender to this simple truth. God loves me and you equally. How then can there be victory or loss for either of us?

In the place of games of guilt, let me remember that I am innocent and so are you. Whatever I have done to you, whatever you have done to me, is forgiven. Indeed, in God's eyes, it never existed. It is but the illusion of our play.

Attack, murder, rape, abuse of any kind — do you think God understands these things? Do you think these acts of desperation are real to the King of Love?

If so, He would respond with a vengeance, raining down fire and ripping the flesh, punishing us for our sins. But, in so doing, He would cease to be a God of love. Truth would become relative. Violence would belong to God, and so become our inheritance.

Are we children of an angry God? If so, we shall not be saved from this vale of tears. If so, the illusion is all there is.

What you believe of God, you believe of yourself and your brother or sister. That must be clearly seen.

If you set evil above you in the shape of God, you set it below you as sin, and guilt and shame, and you encounter it in all of the faces you meet as you walk through life.

Would you walk with evil or with good? That is the choice you make. One choice confirms the illusion. The other pierces the veil and brings you to truth.

Living in the consciousness of God's love is understanding that nothing bad ever happens to you, because how could anything bad happen to God's daughter or son? In truth, it is not possible.

Things happen that seem to be bad, but I do not know what they mean. I am not capable of judging them. I am innocent and free. For the one who knows guides me through this day, this hour, this moment of tears or quiet grief.

Something bad seems to happen, and I find myself wanting to take the blame or wanting to give it to you, but I see that it's just my mind on automatic pilot, trying to evaluate what is neither good nor bad. So I just let it be. I do not deny. I do not justify. I just allow everything to be exactly as it is. And I say "show me the way back home. I have lost my peace."

My life is a prayer for peace. My life is a prayer for truth. In the apparent absence of love, I call for love unashamedly. For love is what I want and love is what I need.

Blessed be each one of us, for we walk slowly toward the light. Through the dark places, we walk. Through our pain, we walk.

Through our grief and our shame and our suffering, we walk.

This is our journey through darkness. We approach the moment of first light with the trust that calls it into being. The Lover calls to the Beloved, and the Beloved appears. The Beloved appears, carrying us on her back, and next to her our Father, the light-bearer himself, leading the way out of darkness.

Mistakes linger but draw forgiveness in the end. The stain is washed away by the tide of acceptance and love. This is the "journey without distance," the journey without beginning or end. For "love does not condemn," but reminds us that we were always free. Free to learn and free to forgive.

It is not the outer shell that matters, but what is inside. And inside the form is a gentle presence that says: "this is my son or daughter in whom I am well pleased." Inside the form is the unconditional love that holds the universe in place, the love that makes flowers unfold in the spring air and the waves endlessly reach for the shore. Inside the form is what extends through it, like a breath, breathing us, loving us, surrendering us to itself.

There is but one flower, one ocean, one thought. And we all belong to it, now and forever. Let us remember this.

Let us remember.

Namaste.

Paul Ferrini is the author of over 40 books on love, healing and forgiveness. His unique blend of spirituality and psychology goes beyond self-help and recovery into the heart of healing. His conferences, retreats, and *Affinity Group Process* have helped thousands of people deepen their practice of forgiveness and open their hearts to the divine presence in themselves and others.

For more information on Paul's work, visit the website at *www.paulferrini.com*. The website has many excerpts from Paul Ferrini's books, as well as information on his workshops and retreats. Be sure to request Paul's free email newsletter, as well as a free catalog of his books and audio products. You can also email: info@**heartwayspress.com** or write to **Heartways Press, 9 Phillips Steet, Greenfield, MA 01301.**

The Long-Awaited Roadmap to Self-Healing and Empowerment

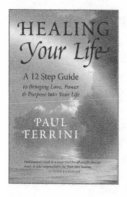

Healing Your Life
12 Steps to Heal Your Childhood Wounds and Bring Love, Power & Purpose into Your Life

BY PAUL FERRINI
ISBN: 978-1-879159-85-3
176 Pages   Paperback $14.95

Paul Ferrini finally shares his powerful 12-Step Roadmap to healing and transformation. This work is the fruit of 35 years of writing and teaching experience.

This book will help you open up to a life of genuine healing and empowerment. You can learn to love yourself from the inside out, initiating a process of giving and receiving that will transform your life. You can end your suffering and connect with your joy. You can find your passion in life and learn to nurture and express your gifts. You can learn to be the bringer of love to your own experience and attract more and more love into your life. You can fulfill your life purpose and live with your partner in an equal, mutually empowered relationship. All the gifts of life and love are possible for you. You need only do your part and open your heart to receive them.

"35 years of heart-centered spiritual work have taught me what is necessary to bring about a real, lasting change in a person's consciousness and experience."

— PAUL FERRINI

The Keys to the Kingdom
8 Spiritual Practices that will Transform Your Life

BY PAUL FERRINI
ISBN: 978-1-879159-84-6
128 Pages   Paperback $12.95

8 SPIRITUAL PRACTICES THAT WILL TRANSFORM YOUR LIFE

1. *Love Yourself*
2. *Be Yourself*
3. *Be Responsible*
4. *Be Honest*
5. *Walk Your Talk*
6. *Follow Your Heart*
7. *Be at Peace*
8. *Stay Present*

Please use the keys in this book to open the doorways in your life. Take the keys with you wherever you go. Use them as often as you can. They will help you to transform your experience. Fear will drop away and unconditional love will shine through. As you awaken to who you are, so will the people around you.

A fearful world cannot exist for a loving heart. Love changes everything. That is why this works. Do your part, and you will see for yourself.

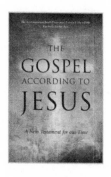
If you know me in your heart, you embody my teaching with an inner certainty. You know that love is the only answer to your problems.

When you give love you cannot help but receive it. Indeed, the more you give, the more you receive. There is no deficiency of love in the world. Love lives in the heart of every human being. If it is trusted, it has the power to uplift consciousness and change the conditions under which you live.

Love is ultimate reality. It is the beginning and the end, the alpha and the omega. It emanates from itself, expresses itself and rests in itself. Whether rising or falling, waxing or waning, ebbing or flowing, it never loses touch with what it is.

I may not be present here in a body, but I am present in your love. When you find the love in your heart, you know that I am with you. It is that simple.

New Book by Paul Ferrini

The long-awaited sequel to *Dancing with the Beloved*

When Love Comes as a Gift
Meeting the Soul Mate in this Life
BY PAUL FERRINI
ISBN: 978-1-879159-81-5
176 Pages Paperback $12.95
ebook $10.00

The soul mate is not just one person, but a work in progress, a tapestry being woven out of light and shadow, hope and fear. Every lover we have prepares us to meet the Beloved. Each one brings a lesson and a gift and each defers to another who brings a deeper gift and a more compelling lesson.

Our partner challenges us to become authentic and emotionally present. S/he invites us to walk through our fears, to tell the truth and to trust more deeply. Gradually, we open our hearts to the potential of creating intimacy on all levels.

And then it is no longer a temporal affair. It is Spirit come to flesh. It is the indwelling Presence of Love, blessing us and lifting us up. It is both a gift and a responsibility, both a promise made and a promise fulfilled.

New Audio by Paul Ferrini

Freedom from Self-Betrayal
Spiritual Mastery Talks at Palm Island

6 CDs $59.95   ISBN 978-1-879159-87-7

Putting Flesh on the Bones
Aligning our Worldly Life with our Spiritual Purpose
Recordings from the 2009 Retreat in
Santa Fe, New Mexico
5 CDs $49.00   ISBN 978-1-879159-80-8

Real Happiness
Awakening To Our True Self
An Introductory Talk by Paul Ferrini
1 CD $16.95   ISBN 978-1-879159-75-4

Roadmap to Real Happiness
Living the Life of Joy and Purpose
You Were Meant to Live
Part 1 4 CDs $48.00   ISBN 978-1-879159-72-3

Part 2 3 CDs $36.00
ISBN 978-1-879159-73-0

Creating a Life of Fulfillment
Insights on Work, Relationship and Life Purpose
2 CDs $24.95
ISBN 978-1-879159-76-1

New Audio Releases

Being an Instrument of Love in Times of Planetary Crisis
Two Talks on Individual and Collective Healing
2 CDs $24.95   ISBN 978-1-879159-79-2

The Radiant Light Within
Readings by Paul Ferrini from the *Hidden Jewel* & *Dancing with the Beloved*
1 CD $16.95   ISBN 978-1-879159-74-7

Audio Books

The Economy of Love Readings from *Silence of the Heart, The Ecstatic Moment, Grace Unfolding* and other books.
ISBN 1-879159-56-2 $16.95

Relationship as a Spiritual Path Readings from *Creating a Spiritual Relationship, Dancing with the Beloved, Miracle of Love* and other books. ISBN 1-879159-55-4 $16.95

The Hands of God Readings from *Illuminations, Enlightenment for Everyone, Forbidden Fruit, The Great Way of All Beings* and other books. ISBN 1-879159-57-0 $16.95

Heart and Soul
Poems of Love and Awakening read by the Author.
ISBN 978-1-879159-77-8   1 CD $16.95

Audio Workshops on CD

Seeds of Transformation:
Set includes: *Healing Without Fixing, The Wound and the Gift, Opening to the Divine Love Energy, The Laws of Love, The Path to Mastery.*
5 CDs   ISBN 1-879159-63-5 $48.00

Two Talks on Spiritual Mastery by Paul Ferrini
We are the Bringers of Love   CD 1
Surrendering to What Is   CD 2
2 CDs   ISBN 1-879159-65-1 $24.00

Love is That Certainty
ISBN 1-879159-52-X $16.95

Atonement:
The Awakening of Planet Earth and its Inhabitants
ISBN 1-879159-53-8 $16.95

From Darkness to Light:
The Soul's Journey of Redemption
ISBN 1-879159-54-6 $16.95

Paul Ferrini's Real Happiness Books

Real Happiness
A Roadmap for Healing Our Pain and
Awakening the Joy That Is Our Birthright
160 pages $12.95
ISBN # 978-1-879159-68-6

Embracing Our True Self
A New Paradigm Approach to Healing Our
Wounds, Finding Our Gifts, and Fulfilling Our
Spiritual Purpose
192 pages $13.95
ISBN # 978-1-879159-69-3

**Real Happiness —
The Workbook**
Creating Your Personal Roadmap
to a Joyful and Empowered Life
96 pages $14.95
ISBN # 978-1-879159-71-6

The Hidden Jewel
Discovering the Radiant Light Within
$9.00
ISBN # 978-1-879159-70-9

Paul Ferrini's Course in Spiritual Mastery

Part One: The Laws of Love
A Guide to Living in Harmony
with Universal Spiritual Truth
144 pages $12.95
ISBN # 1-879159-60-0

Part Two: The Power of Love
10 Spiritual Practices that Can Transform Your Life
168 pages $12.95
ISBN # 1-879159-61-9

Part Three: The Presence of Love
God's Answer to Humanity's Call for Help
160 pages $12.95
ISBN # 1-879159-62-7

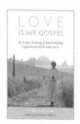

Part Four: Love is My Gospel
The Radical Teachings of Jesus on Healing,
Empowerment and the Call to Serve
128 pages $12.95
ISBN # 1-879159-67-8

Paul's In-depth Presentation of the Laws of Love on 9 CDs

The Laws of Love
Part One (5 CDs) ISBN # 1-879159-58-9 $49.00
Part Two (4 CDs) ISBN # 1-879159-59-7 $39.00

Relationship Books

Dancing with the Beloved:
Opening our Hearts to the Lessons of Love
160 pages paperback $12.95
ISBN 1-879159-47-3

Living in the Heart:
The Affinity Process and the Path of Unconditional
Love and Acceptance
128 pages paperback
ISBN 1-879159-36-8 $10.95

Creating a Spiritual Relationship
128 pages paperback
ISBN 1-879159-39-2 $10.95

The Twelve Steps of Forgiveness
120 pages paperback
ISBN 1-879159-10-4 $10.95

The Ecstatic Moment:
A Practical Manual for Opening Your Heart
and Staying in It
128 pages   paperback
ISBN 1-879159-18-X $10.95

Christ Mind Books and Audio

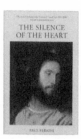
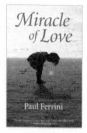

Part 1 Part 2 Part 3 Part 4

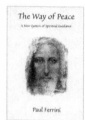
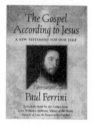

Christ Mind Books

Love Without Conditions ISBN 1-879159-15-5 $12.95
The Silence of the Heart ISBN 1-879159-16-3 $14.95
Miracle of Love ISBN 1-879159-23-6 $12.95
Return to the Garden   ISBN 1-879159-35-x $12.95
The Living Christ ISBN 1-879159-49-X paperback $14.95
I am the Door hardcover ISBN 1-879159-41-4 $21.95
The Way of Peace hardcover ISBN 1-879159-42-2 $19.95

Christ Mind Audio Read by the Author

Love Without Conditions 3 CDs ISBN 978-1-879159-64-8 $36.00

The Gospel According to Jesus
Selected Readings from the Christ Mind Teachings
2CDs ISBN 978-1-879159-78-5 $24.95

Wisdom Books

Everyday Wisdom
A Spiritual Book of Days
224 pages paperback $13.95 ISBN 1-879159-51-1

Wisdom Cards:
Spiritual Guidance for Every Day of our Lives
ISBN 1-879159-50-3 $10.95

Illuminations on the Road to Nowhere
160 pages paperback
ISBN 1-879159-44-9 $12.95

Forbidden Fruit:
Unraveling the Mysteries of Sin, Guilt
and Atonement
ISBN 1-879159-48-1
160 pages paperback $12.95

Enlightenment for Everyone
with an Introduction by Iyanla Vanzant
ISBN 1-879159-45-7
160 pages hardcover $16.00

The Great Way of All Beings:
Renderings of Lao Tzu
ISBN 1-879159-46-5
320 pages hardcover $23.00

Heartways Press Order Form

Name_____

Address_____

City _____State _____Zip_____

Phone/Fax_____ Email* _____

Please include your email to receive Paul's newsletter and weekly wisdom message.

Title ordered	quantity	price
	TOTAL	_____

Priority Shipping: one book $5.95   _____

Additional books, please add $1.50 per book   _____

                                        TOTAL   _____

For shipping outside the USA, or if you require faster delivery,
please contact us for shipping costs.

Fax Order To: Heartways Press 413-774-9475
Or call 413-774-9474 or 941-776-8001
www.PaulFerrini.com   email: orders@heartwayspress.com

Please allow 1–2 weeks for delivery. Payment must be made by credit card (MC/VISA/AmEx) before books are shipped.

Made in the USA
Las Vegas, NV
17 April 2023

70715758R00062